W9-AET-237

The ★ ★
UNITED
STATES
PRESIDENTS

★ ★ Calvin ★ ★

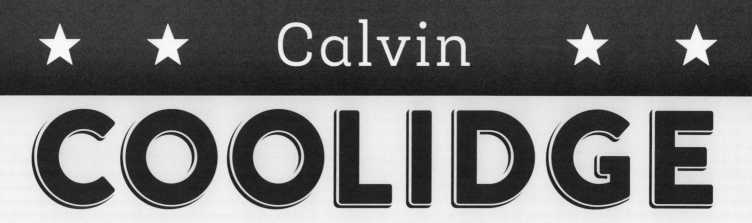

COOLIDGE

Heidi M.D. Elston

Big Buddy Books

An Imprint of Abdo Publishing
abdopublishing.com

abdopublishing.com

Published by Abdo Publishing, a division of ABDO, PO Box 398166, Minneapolis, Minnesota 55439.
Copyright © 2017 by Abdo Consulting Group, Inc. International copyrights reserved in all countries. No
part of this book may be reproduced in any form without written permission from the publisher. Big Buddy
Books™ is a trademark and logo of Abdo Publishing.

Printed in the United States of America, North Mankato, Minnesota
062016
092016

THIS BOOK CONTAINS
RECYCLED MATERIALS

Design: Sarah DeYoung, Mighty Media, Inc.
Production: Mighty Media, Inc.
Editor: Rebecca Felix
Cover Photograph: Getty Images
Interior Photographs: AP Images (pp. 9, 25); Corbis (pp. 7, 15, 17, 23, 27);
    Getty Images (pp. 5, 6, 11, 13, 19, 21, 29)

Cataloging-in-Publication Data

Names: Elston, Heidi M.D., author.
Title: Calvin Coolidge / by Heidi M.D. Elston.
Description: Minneapolis, MN : Abdo Publishing, [2017] | Series: United States
    presidents | Includes bibliographical references and index.
Identifiers: LCCN 2015044095 | ISBN 9781680780901 (lib. bdg.) |
    ISBN 9781680775105 (ebook)
Subjects: LCSH: Coolidge, Calvin, 1872-1933- --Juvenile literature. 2.
    Presidents--United States--Biography--Juvenile literature. | United States--
    Politics and Government--1923-1929--Juvenile literature.
Classification: DDC 973.91/5092092 [B]--dc23
LC record available at http://lccn.loc.gov/2015044095

Contents

Calvin Coolidge

Calvin Coolidge became the thirtieth US president in 1923. Before then, he was active in Massachusetts **politics**. Coolidge was a state **representative** and a state senator. He also became governor.

In 1921, Coolidge became the US vice president. Two years later, President Warren G. Harding died while in office. Coolidge became president. As president, he was honest and hardworking.

Timeline

1872
On July 4, John Calvin Coolidge was born in Plymouth, Vermont.

1912
Coolidge was elected to the Massachusetts state senate.

1906
Coolidge was elected to the Massachusetts House of **Representatives**.

1918
Coolidge was elected governor of Massachusetts.

1923

President Harding died. On August 3, Coolidge became the thirtieth US president.

1921

On March 4, Coolidge became US vice president under Warren G. Harding.

1924

Coolidge was reelected US president.

1933

On January 5, Calvin Coolidge died.

Young Calvin

John Calvin Coolidge was born in Plymouth, Vermont, on July 4, 1872. His parents were John Calvin and Victoria Moor Coolidge. They called their son Calvin. Calvin had a younger sister named Abigail. She was his closest friend.

★ FAST FACTS ★

Born: July 4, 1872

Wife: Grace Anna Goodhue (1879–1957)

Children: two

Political Party: Republican

Age at Inauguration: 51

Years Served: 1923–1929

Vice President: Charles Dawes

Died: January 5, 1933, age 60

Calvin (*standing, second from left*) attended school at Black River Academy in Ludlow, Vermont.

Entering Politics

In 1891, Coolidge entered Amherst College in Amherst, Massachusetts. He completed school in 1895. He then studied law and became a **lawyer** in 1897.

During this time, Coolidge became active in **politics**. He was a **Republican**. In 1898, he was elected to the city council of Northampton, Massachusetts.

In Northampton, Coolidge met Grace Anna Goodhue. The two married on October 4, 1905. The Coolidges had two sons, John and Calvin Jr.

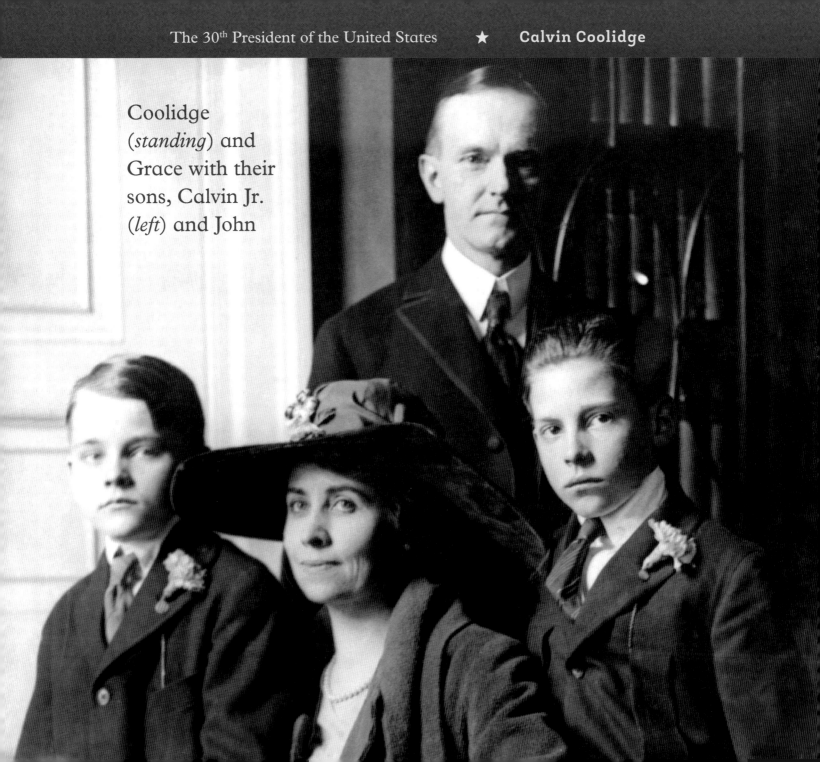

Coolidge (*standing*) and Grace with their sons, Calvin Jr. (*left*) and John

Rising in Politics

Coolidge remained active in **politics**. In 1906, he was elected to the Massachusetts House of **Representatives**. He became mayor of Northampton in 1909.

Coolidge was elected to the Massachusetts state senate in 1912. He later served as senate president for two terms.

Coolidge became lieutenant governor of Massachusetts in 1916. He gave speeches on local and state issues. He was reelected to this position twice.

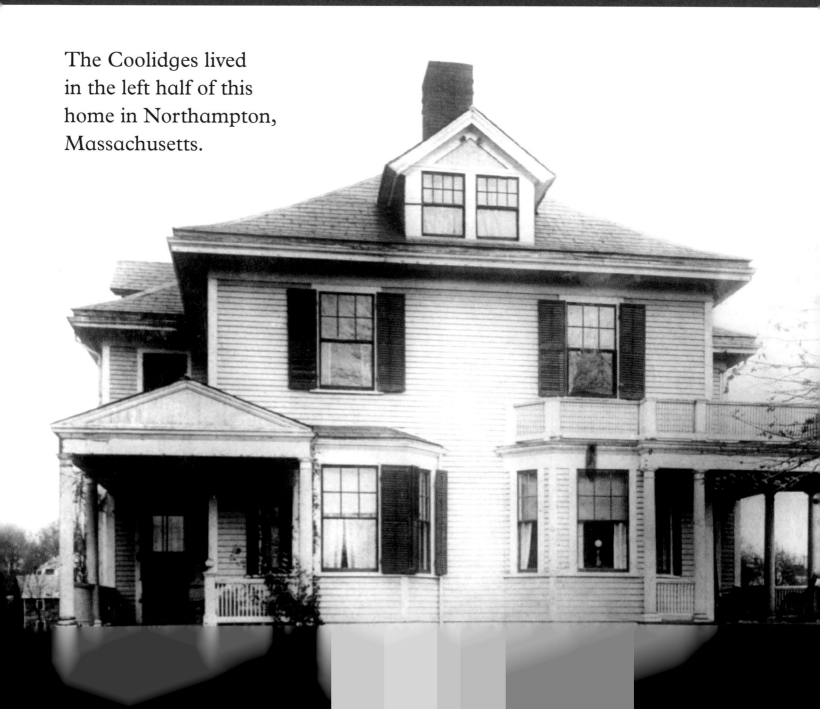

The Coolidges lived in the left half of this home in Northampton, Massachusetts.

Governor Coolidge

In 1918, Coolidge was elected governor of Massachusetts. He took office on January 1, 1919. On September 9 of that year, more than 1,100 of the 1,500 Boston, Massachusetts, police officers went on strike. Two days of disorder followed.

Coolidge called in the state guard to control the city. The police commissioner decided the striking officers would lose their jobs. Coolidge agreed. Americans **praised** the governor's firm stand. Coolidge was reelected by a record vote in the 1919 election.

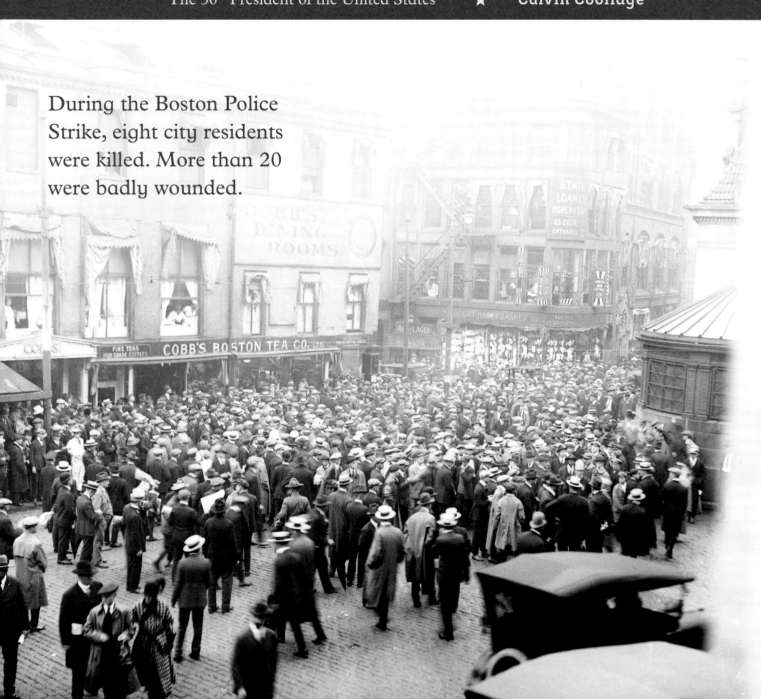

During the Boston Police Strike, eight city residents were killed. More than 20 were badly wounded.

New President

In 1920, Warren G. Harding ran for president. Coolidge ran as his vice president. Coolidge and Harding won the race.

Harding was **inaugurated** the twenty-ninth US president on March 4, 1921. Coolidge became vice president that day.

One summer night in 1923, Coolidge was awoken with shocking news. President Harding had died. Coolidge would become president. On August 3, he was inaugurated by his father, a **notary public**.

John Calvin Coolidge inaugurating his son. Never before in US history had a president been inaugurated by his father.

Cleaning House

Harding's **administration** had been filled with many dishonest people. Other government officials feared these people were lying to the nation. Coolidge hired **lawyers** to find out.

The lawyers brought to court anyone that took part in **political** crimes. Americans liked Coolidge's firm leadership. He brought back their trust in government.

Coolidge reduced certain taxes. He also kept government spending low. As a result, Coolidge cut the national **debt** by about $1 **billion** a year.

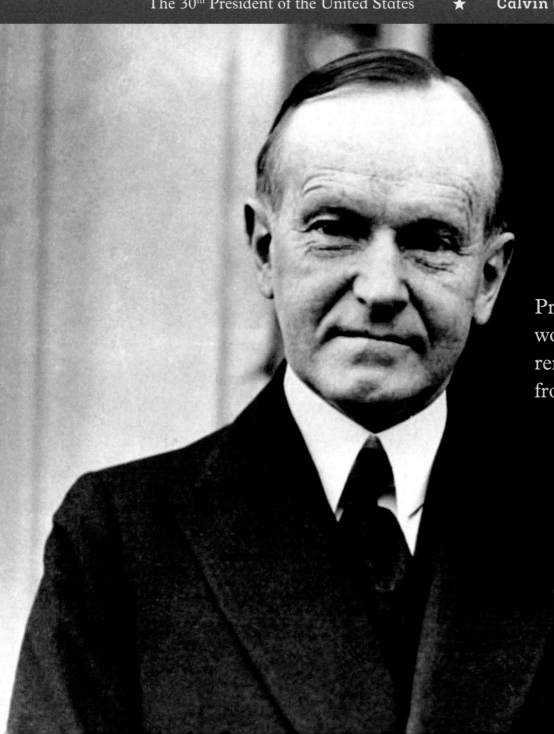

President Coolidge worked hard to quickly remove all dishonesty from the White House.

Reelection

In 1924, 16-year-old Calvin Jr. died of a foot **infection**. Coolidge suffered from this loss. He was tired and sad. Yet he entered the 1924 election for president. Charles Dawes was Coolidge's **running mate**.

Coolidge's **slogan** was "Keep Cool with Coolidge." Americans were happy with his leadership. He easily won the election.

SUPREME COURT APPOINTMENT

Harlan Fiske Stone: 1925

Coolidge's running mate, Charles Dawes, was the US Bureau of the Budget director.

President Coolidge

Coolidge was **inaugurated** on March 4, 1925. He kept his stand on taxes and spending. The **economy** continued to grow.

Congress tried to pass the McNary-Haugen bill. It would help farmers get out of **debt**. But Coolidge worried the bill would raise prices for buyers. So, he stopped the bill.

Coolidge **supported** the Kellogg-Briand Pact in 1928. This agreement prevented using war to settle arguments between countries.

President Coolidge signing
the Kellogg-Briand Pact

Coolidge Prosperity

Under Coolidge's leadership, big US businesses grew even larger. Factories shipped huge amounts of goods. Sales of buildings and land in nearly every town boomed.

Many workers enjoyed higher pay. They had a shorter workweek too. Some workers even received paid vacations.

However, not everyone benefited under Coolidge **prosperity**. Farmers suffered greatly. Their crop prices fell, and they sold less in **foreign** markets.

PRESIDENT COOLIDGE'S CABINET

Coolidge (*seated, third from left*) with his cabinet in 1927

First Term
August 3, 1923–March 4, 1925

★ **STATE:** Charles Evans Hughes
★ **TREASURY:** Andrew W. Mellon
★ **WAR:** John Wingate Weeks
★ **NAVY:** Edwin Denby,
Curtis Dwight Wilbur (from March 18, 1924)
★ **ATTORNEY GENERAL:** Harry Micajah Daugherty,
Harlan Fiske Stone (from April 9, 1924)
★ **INTERIOR:** Hubert Work
★ **AGRICULTURE:** Henry Cantwell Wallace,
Howard Mason Gore (from November 21, 1924)
★ **COMMERCE:** Herbert Hoover
★ **LABOR:** James John Davis

Second Term
March 4, 1925–March 4, 1929

★ **STATE:** Frank B. Kellogg
★ **TREASURY:** Andrew W. Mellon
★ **WAR:** John Wingate Weeks,
Dwight F. Davis (from October 14, 1925)
★ **NAVY:** Curtis Dwight Wilbur
★ **ATTORNEY GENERAL:** John Garibaldi Sargent
★ **INTERIOR:** Hubert Work,
Roy Owen West (from January 21, 1929)
★ **AGRICULTURE:** William Marion Jardine
★ **COMMERCE:** Herbert Hoover,
William Fairfield Whiting (from December 11, 1928)
★ **LABOR:** James John Davis

25

Coolidge Goes Home

Coolidge chose not to run for president in the 1928 election. He left the White House in March 1929. Coolidge **retired** to Northampton.

Coolidge spent time with his family in Northampton. He wrote magazine and newspaper articles. He also wrote a book about his life.

The Coolidges soon moved to a home in Northampton called The Beeches. It gave them privacy. There, gates kept **tourists** from getting too close.

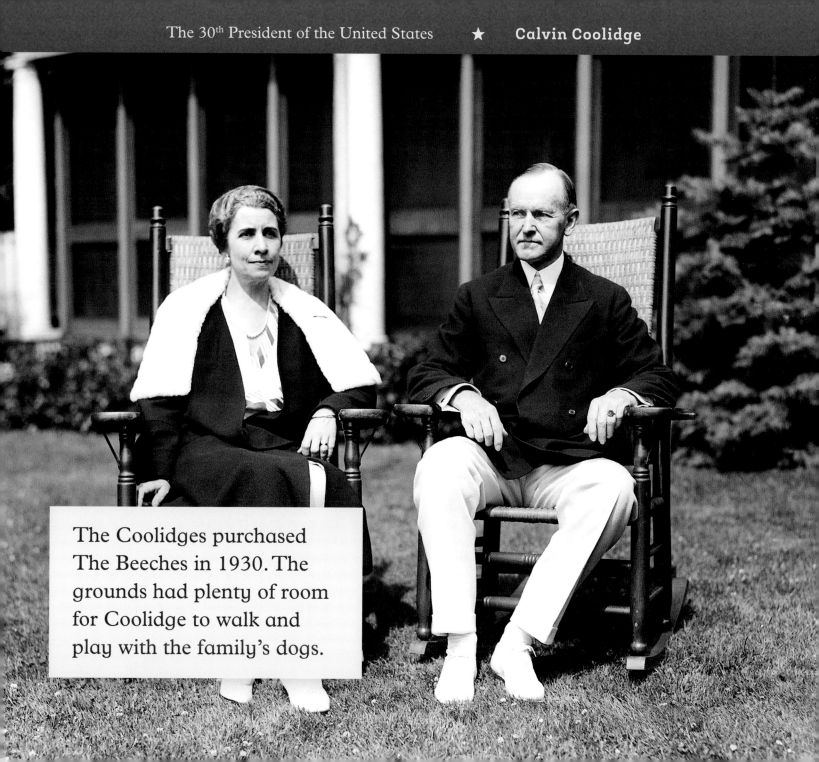

The Coolidges purchased The Beeches in 1930. The grounds had plenty of room for Coolidge to walk and play with the family's dogs.

In October 1929, the US **economy** failed. Many Americans lost their jobs. This was the beginning of the **Great Depression**.

Many people had **praised** Coolidge while he was president. Now, those same people blamed him for America's troubles. They felt he could have done more to prevent the depression.

On January 5, 1933, Calvin Coolidge died of a heart attack. He was buried beside his father and son.

Coolidge worked hard for his country. He believed actions were more powerful than words. He helped Americans trust in government again.

Coolidge was a shy, quiet man who rarely smiled. He was known as "Silent Cal."

Office of the President

Branches of Government

The US government has three branches. They are the executive, legislative, and judicial branches. Each branch has some power over the others. This is called a system of checks and balances.

★ Executive Branch

The executive branch enforces laws. It is made up of the president, the vice president, and the president's cabinet. The president represents the United States around the world. He or she also signs bills into law and leads the military.

★ Legislative Branch

The legislative branch makes laws, maintains the military, and regulates trade. It also has the power to declare war. This branch includes the Senate and the House of Representatives. Together, these two houses form Congress.

★ Judicial Branch

The judicial branch interprets laws. It is made up of district courts, courts of appeals, and the Supreme Court. District courts try cases. Sometimes people disagree with a trial's outcome. Then he or she may appeal. If a court of appeals supports the ruling, a person may appeal to the Supreme Court.

Qualifications for Office

To be president, a candidate must be at least 35 years old. The person must be a natural-born US citizen. He or she must also have lived in the United States for at least 14 years.

Electoral College

The US presidential election is an indirect election. Voters from each state choose electors. These electors represent their state in the Electoral College. Each elector has one electoral vote. Electors cast their vote for the candidate with the highest number of votes from people in their state. A candidate must receive the majority of Electoral College votes to win.

Term of Office

Each president may be elected to two four-year terms. The presidential election is held on the Tuesday after the first Monday in November. The president is sworn in on January 20 of the following year. At that time, he or she takes the oath of office. It states:

> I do solemnly swear (or affirm) that I will faithfully execute the office of President of the United States, and will to the best of my ability, preserve, protect and defend the Constitution of the United States.

Line of Succession

The Presidential Succession Act of 1947 states who becomes president if the president cannot serve. The vice president is first in the line. Next are the Speaker of the House and the President Pro Tempore of the Senate. It may happen that none of these individuals is able to serve. Then the office falls to the president's cabinet members. They would take office in the order in which each department was created:

Secretary of State

Secretary of the Treasury

Secretary of Defense

Attorney General

Secretary of the Interior

Secretary of Agriculture

Secretary of Commerce

Secretary of Labor

Secretary of Health and Human Services

Secretary of Housing
   and Urban Development

Secretary of Transportation

Secretary of Energy

Secretary of Education

Secretary of Veterans Affairs

Secretary of Homeland Security

Benefits

★ While in office, the president receives a salary. It is $400,000 per year. He or she lives in the White House. The president also has 24-hour Secret Service protection.

★ The president may travel on a Boeing 747 jet. This special jet is called Air Force One. It can hold 70 passengers. It has kitchens, a dining room, sleeping areas, and more. Air Force One can fly halfway around the world before needing to refuel. It can even refuel in flight!

★ When the president travels by car, he or she uses Cadillac One. It is a Cadillac Deville that has been modified. The car has heavy armor and communications systems. The president may even take Cadillac One along when visiting other countries.

★ The president also travels on a helicopter. It is called Marine One. It may also be taken along when the president visits other countries.

★ Sometimes the president needs to get away with family and friends. Camp David is the official presidential retreat. It is located in Maryland. The US Navy maintains the retreat. The US Marine Corps keeps it secure. The camp offers swimming, tennis, golf, and hiking.

★ When the president leaves office, he or she receives lifetime Secret Service protection. He or she also receives a yearly pension of $203,700. The former president also receives money for office space, supplies, and staff.

PRESIDENTS AND THEIR TERMS

PRESIDENT	PARTY	TOOK OFFICE	LEFT OFFICE	TERMS SERVED	VICE PRESIDENT
George Washington	None	April 30, 1789	March 4, 1797	Two	John Adams
John Adams	Federalist	March 4, 1797	March 4, 1801	One	Thomas Jefferson
Thomas Jefferson	Democratic-Republican	March 4, 1801	March 4, 1809	Two	Aaron Burr, George Clinton
James Madison	Democratic-Republican	March 4, 1809	March 4, 1817	Two	George Clinton, Elbridge Gerry
James Monroe	Democratic-Republican	March 4, 1817	March 4, 1825	Two	Daniel D. Tompkins
John Quincy Adams	Democratic-Republican	March 4, 1825	March 4, 1829	One	John C. Calhoun
Andrew Jackson	Democrat	March 4, 1829	March 4, 1837	Two	John C. Calhoun, Martin Van Buren
Martin Van Buren	Democrat	March 4, 1837	March 4, 1841	One	Richard M. Johnson
William H. Harrison	Whig	March 4, 1841	April 4, 1841	Died During First Term	John Tyler
John Tyler	Whig	April 6, 1841	March 4, 1845	Completed Harrison's Term	Office Vacant
James K. Polk	Democrat	March 4, 1845	March 4, 1849	One	George M. Dallas
Zachary Taylor	Whig	March 5, 1849	July 9, 1850	Died During First Term	Millard Fillmore

PRESIDENT	PARTY	TOOK OFFICE	LEFT OFFICE	TERMS SERVED	VICE PRESIDENT
Millard Fillmore	Whig	July 10, 1850	March 4, 1853	Completed Taylor's Term	Office Vacant
Franklin Pierce	Democrat	March 4, 1853	March 4, 1857	One	William R.D. King
James Buchanan	Democrat	March 4, 1857	March 4, 1861	One	John C. Breckinridge
Abraham Lincoln	Republican	March 4, 1861	April 15, 1865	Served One Term, Died During Second Term	Hannibal Hamlin, Andrew Johnson
Andrew Johnson	Democrat	April 15, 1865	March 4, 1869	Completed Lincoln's Second Term	Office Vacant
Ulysses S. Grant	Republican	March 4, 1869	March 4, 1877	Two	Schuyler Colfax, Henry Wilson
Rutherford B. Hayes	Republican	March 3, 1877	March 4, 1881	One	William A. Wheeler
James A. Garfield	Republican	March 4, 1881	September 19, 1881	Died During First Term	Chester Arthur
Chester Arthur	Republican	September 20, 1881	March 4, 1885	Completed Garfield's Term	Office Vacant
Grover Cleveland	Democrat	March 4, 1885	March 4, 1889	One	Thomas A. Hendricks
Benjamin Harrison	Republican	March 4, 1889	March 4, 1893	One	Levi P. Morton
Grover Cleveland	Democrat	March 4, 1893	March 4, 1897	One	Adlai E. Stevenson
William McKinley	Republican	March 4, 1897	September 14, 1901	Served One Term, Died During Second Term	Garret A. Hobart, Theodore Roosevelt

PRESIDENT	PARTY	TOOK OFFICE	LEFT OFFICE	TERMS SERVED	VICE PRESIDENT
Theodore Roosevelt	Republican	September 14, 1901	March 4, 1909	Completed McKinley's Second Term, Served One Term	Office Vacant, Charles Fairbanks
William Taft	Republican	March 4, 1909	March 4, 1913	One	James S. Sherman
Woodrow Wilson	Democrat	March 4, 1913	March 4, 1921	Two	Thomas R. Marshall
Warren G. Harding	Republican	March 4, 1921	August 2, 1923	Died During First Term	Calvin Coolidge
Calvin Coolidge	Republican	August 3, 1923	March 4, 1929	Completed Harding's Term, Served One Term	Office Vacant, Charles Dawes
Herbert Hoover	Republican	March 4, 1929	March 4, 1933	One	Charles Curtis
Franklin D. Roosevelt	Democrat	March 4, 1933	April 12, 1945	Served Three Terms, Died During Fourth Term	John Nance Garner, Henry A. Wallace, Harry S. Truman
Harry S. Truman	Democrat	April 12, 1945	January 20, 1953	Completed Roosevelt's Fourth Term, Served One Term	Office Vacant, Alben Barkley
Dwight D. Eisenhower	Republican	January 20, 1953	January 20, 1961	Two	Richard Nixon
John F. Kennedy	Democrat	January 20, 1961	November 22, 1963	Died During First Term	Lyndon B. Johnson
Lyndon B. Johnson	Democrat	November 22, 1963	January 20, 1969	Completed Kennedy's Term, Served One Term	Office Vacant, Hubert H. Humphrey
Richard Nixon	Republican	January 20, 1969	August 9, 1974	Completed First Term, Resigned During Second Term	Spiro T. Agnew, Gerald Ford

PRESIDENT	PARTY	TOOK OFFICE	LEFT OFFICE	TERMS SERVED	VICE PRESIDENT
Gerald Ford	Republican	August 9, 1974	January 20, 1977	Completed Nixon's Second Term	Nelson A. Rockefeller
Jimmy Carter	Democrat	January 20, 1977	January 20, 1981	One	Walter Mondale
Ronald Reagan	Republican	January 20, 1981	January 20, 1989	Two	George H.W. Bush
George H.W. Bush	Republican	January 20, 1989	January 20, 1993	One	Dan Quayle
Bill Clinton	Democrat	January 20, 1993	January 20, 2001	Two	Al Gore
George W. Bush	Republican	January 20, 2001	January 20, 2009	Two	Dick Cheney
Barack Obama	Democrat	January 20, 2009	January 20, 2017	Two	Joe Biden

"It is always important to do the right thing." Calvin Coolidge

★ WRITE TO THE PRESIDENT ★

You may write to the president at:
The White House
1600 Pennsylvania Avenue NW
Washington, DC 20500

You may e-mail the president at:
comments@whitehouse.gov

37

Glossary

administration (uhd-mih-nuh-STRAY-shuhn)—a group of people that manages an operation, a department, or an office.

billion—a very large number that equals one thousand million.

debt—something owed to someone else, especially money.

economy—the way that a country produces, sells, and buys goods and services.

foreign—located outside one's own country.

Great Depression—the period from 1929 to 1942 of worldwide economic trouble. There was little buying and selling, and many people could not find work.

inaugurate (ih-NAW-gyuh-rayt)—to swear into a political office.

infection (ihn-FEHK-shuhn)—the causing of an unhealthy condition by something harmful, such as bacteria.

lawyer (LAW-yuhr)—a person who gives people advice on laws or represents them in court.

notary public—a public officer authorized to record the fact that a certain person swears that something is true, and to attend to other legal matters.

politics—the art or science of government. Something referring to politics is political. A person who is active in politics is a politician.

praise—to give approval or admiration.

prosperity—the state of being successful, usually by making a lot of money.

representative—someone chosen in an election to act or speak for the people who voted for him or her.

Republican—a member of the Republican political party.

retire—to give up one's job.

running mate—someone running for vice president with another person running for president in an election.

slogan—a word or a phrase used to express a position, a stand, or a goal.

support—to believe in or be in favor of something.

tourist—a person who travels for pleasure.

★ WEBSITES ★

To learn more about the US Presidents, visit **booklinks.abdopublishing.com**. These links are routinely monitored and updated to provide the most current information available.

39

Index

LIBRARY

Atlanta-Fulton Public Library

R4003076686

J B COOLIDGE

Elston, Heidi M. D.
Calvin Coolidge

DISCARD